William Henry Smith

Charles Hammond and his relations to Henry Clay and John Quincy Adams 1884

Constitutional limitations and the contest for freedom of speech and the

press

William Henry Smith

Charles Hammond and his relations to Henry Clay and John Quincy Adams 1884
Constitutional limitations and the contest for freedom of speech and the press

ISBN/EAN: 9783337278656

Printed in Europe, USA, Canada, Australia, Japan

Cover: Foto ©Suzi / pixelio.de

More available books at **www.hansebooks.com**

CHARLES HAMMOND

AND

His Relations to Henry Clay and John Quincy Adams

OR

ITUTIONAL LIMITATIONS AND THE CONTEST
)R FREEDOM OF SPEECH AND THE PRESS

An Address delivered before the Chicago Historical
Society, May 20, 1884

By WM. HENRY SMITH

———

Published for the Chicago Historical Society
1885

TO

ROBERT CLARKE, ESQ.

AS A RECOGNITION OF HIS INTELLIGENT EFFORTS TO ENLARGE

THE SCOPE OF AMERICAN HISTORY, OF HIS PATRIOTISM

AS A CITIZEN, AND OF GENIAL AND MANLY TRAITS

THAT ARE ADMIRED BY HIS FRIENDS.

CHICAGO HISTORICAL SOCIETY.

PROCEEDINGS OF A MEETING HELD MAY 20, 1884.

An adjourned quarterly meeting of the Society was held May 20, 1884. Vice President E. B. Washburne occupied the chair. From the Librarian's Report it appeared that the accessions to the Library during the quarter were 226 bound volumes and 170 unbound books and pamphlets.

Judge Mark Skinner introduced the following tribute to the memory of the late President of the Society, Hon. I. N. Arnold, which was unanimously adopted:

"*Resolved*, 1st, In the removal by death of the Hon. Isaac N. Arnold, the Historical Society mourns the loss of one of its original founders, of one of its most active, efficient, and reliable members, and its honored and greatly respected President.

" During all the active years of a brief and well-spent life, Mr. Arnold has been a citizen of Chicago, contributing by his indefatigable industry, unimpeachable integrity, his patriotism, his public spirit, his rare abilities, his great acquirements, his spotless moral character, his high qualifications, and his instincts as a thorough gentleman, to give luster to the city, his residence, and to the generation to which he belonged.

"A successful lawyer, that stood in the front rank of his profession, a cautious, far-seeing and wise legislator, distinguishing

(*v*)

himself in the halls of legislation, as well national as state, a successful public speaker, and a writer of great power and widespread popularity. he has left to the generations that succeed him the legacy of a noble example and a good name; therefore,

"*Resolved*, 2nd, That the Hon. E. B. Washburne be requested to prepare and deliver before this Society, at his convenience, a memorial address commemorative of the life and character of the Hon. Isaac N. Arnold."

Mr. Washburne responded to the resolution as follows:

"I am certain that all the members of the Chicago Historical Society, and all others present, will have heard with emotion the resolution in respect to our President.

"The Society has met with a great and almost irreparable loss in the death of Mr. Arnold. Long identified with it, giving to it his attention and his services, he has done much to elevate its character and increase its usefulness. We can never forget with what courtesy and dignity he presided at our meetings. Dying, as it were, in the harness, he has left to us the recollection of an honest man, a cultivated gentleman, a good citizen, and an honored public servant. At some time in the future, the Society will pay appropriate honors to his memory."

Hon. William Bross was requested by the Society to prepare and read before it a memorial notice of the late Thomas H. Armstrong, who was for some time the Secretary and Treasurer of this Society.

Mr. E. H. Sheldon introduced the following memorial notice of the late Sir Alpheus Todd, which was unanimously adopted and ordered spread upon the records:

"Sir Alpheus Todd, late of Ottawa. Canada, was born in England in 1821. and at the age of twelve emigrated to Canada. In 1856 he became Librarian of the Legislative Assembly of Canada and held the position till the time of his death. In 1866 Mr. Todd was elected a corresponding member of this Society. He wrote several works, which were highly commended, relating to the government of Canada and England. The ability and noble manhood exhibited in Mr. Todd's works won for him the honor of knighthood and the high esteem of those who knew him.

"As a mark of respect, this Society places his name with the honored dead upon its records."

The President appointed Messrs. E. H. Sheldon, Mark Skinner, and W. K. Ackerman a committee to draft resolutions of respect to the memory of the late Cyrus H. McCormick, an annual member of this Society.

The President then introduced Mr. Wm. Henry Smith, who read the following historical paper upon "Charles Hammond and his relations to Henry Clay and John Quincy Adams."

Upon the address being concluded, General A. L. Chetlain moved that the thanks of this Society be tendered to Mr. Smith for his excellent historical paper, and a request was made that he furnish the Society a copy for its archives. The motion was unanimously adopted and the meeting adjourned.

ALBERT D. HAGER, *Secretary.*

CHARLES HAMMOND.

In the winter of 1860–1, on the eve of the great civil war, I heard that brilliant Democratic orator, Ex-Senator Geo. E. Pugh, declare to an audience that filled the old Smith & Nixon's Hall, and embraced the intelligence and wealth of Cincinnati, that if the differences between the North and South resulted in war, the commerce of Cincinnati would be destroyed, grass would grow in her streets, and the glory of the Queen City would depart forever. The eloquent Senator doubtless expressed his honest convictions; he certainly did express the opinion of a large number of the business men of that city. Considerations of patriotism, of legal rights, and of manhood, did not enter into their thoughts. The only question was, how could the trade of the South be preserved for Cincinnati? These merchants thought most surely by asking the South to write the terms on which they would consent to remain in the Union, and continue to govern the country. They called this conservatism—a word often representing "wisdom in the administration of affairs. But there is conservatism and conservatism. This of the eventful period preceding the war, was what Carlyle would have called "slothful cowardice," but what may be more accurately described as the conservatism of cowardice—destructive of the soul.

This was but the echo of other days. The fathers of many there present had heard a similar prediction from the lips of a distinguished citizen (sometime justice of the Supreme Court, and United States Senator), if the subject of slavery were even permitted to be discussed by the press north of the Ohio river, and in this opinion there seemed to be for a season an almost universal concurrence. There was, however, one man, in that day the most eminent of the citizens of Ohio or of the West, who controverted that opinion, and who continued to discuss the subject of slavery, its relations to society and the state, despite the passionate remonstrances of friends, and in the face of mobs, with sublime courage, and a calmness and wisdom that disarmed the violent and carried conviction to thousands. This was the conservatism of life—the power of truth that ever has and ever will put the devil to flight.

The ghost of a controversy is haunting the present generation, seeking to be laid when it shall be determined who first proposed immediate emancipation. What does it matter? Gradual emancipation at one time, through restrictive measures was practicable; but the conservatism of cowardice had permitted greed and lust for power to so far override the spirit of the Constitution as to fasten the evil of slavery firmly upon the Union, so that emancipation, except by the sword, was impracticable. It has come to be fashionable to seek for heroes supposed to be, in the days when there was a shadow over the land, the sole keepers of the conscience of the Republic. Bronze monuments are erected in memory, and verses are sung by immortal bards in honor of men (a few impracticables) who denounced the Constitution as "a covenant with death, and an agreement with hell." Forgotten are the wise men, who abhorring wrong, addressed themselves to the task of securing the amelioration of slavery through practicable means under the Constitution. The venerable Franklin petitioning for the restriction of slavery at the seat of government by legal enactment; Charles Hammond, insisting that slavery should be discussed with the same freedom as any other question affecting the welfare of society; John Quincy Adams in the midst of a storm of passions asserting the right of petition; and Owen Lovejoy, defending his press with his life, are figures that stand out boldly in the history of this great moral contest, and challenge the grateful admiration of the American people. Their influence was the power that created a healthy public opinion; it was the influence of a noble manhood. Yet they did not indulge in idle denunciation. They labored to give to the people an intelligent and just appreciation of their own rights, and to establish the true relations of the states to each other under the Constitution, which they believed, as we believe to-day, was and is the most beneficent instrument of government ever devised by man. Passion may serve as a spur, but it is the judgment intrenched in conviction that endures in the hour of trial, and commands success.

Pardon this long prologue. It seemed necessary to properly introduce my subject. Perhaps it may not be unprofitable to draw the line between those who receive and those who deserve the mead of praise.

I am to speak to you to-night of the career of Charles Hammond, a famous man in his time, who conferred honor upon two professions, and left the world richer for his having lived. The American people are greatly indebted to him. As we have chiefly to do with public affairs, I shall omit details of Hammond's early life, merely remarking by way of introduction, that he was born near Baltimore, Maryland, September 19, 1779. His parents, George and Elizabeth Wells Hammond, belonged to the Episcopal Church, were well educated and noted for strong traits of character. With their help and that of a tutor in mathematics and Latin, Charles received the basis of that thorough culture which he afterwards acquired.

There are men who are superior mentally, and to whom the extrinsic aids afforded by a thorough college course do not seem to be necessary. Charles Hammond was of this class. There is little in journalistic or periodical writing equal to his for directness, simplicity, and beauty of diction; or in the productions of the Bar, in logical force and perspicuity. His printed legal arguments, we are assured by an admiring contemporary, were the pride and delight of the Bar in his day. One of these, I chanced to find among some rubbish fifteen years ago, with the title page missing, and no mark to indicate the author. It was an argument in criticism of the opinion of Chief Justice Mashall, in Wayman *v.* Southard, in 1825. So perfect was the construction, and so direct and natural the argument, that I said there were not more than two men in the United States who could have written that, and one of them was Hammond, and bore the precious document away and had it bound with Hammond's name. Since then in letters to Henry Clay and Judge Wright, I found the authorship avowed.

" Hammond spoke at the Bar," said the venerable Thomas Ewing three or four years before his death, " Hammond spoke at the Bar as good English as Addison wrote in the Spectator." And Ex-Justice Swayne remarked to me recently that, "It was Mr. Hammond's habit to argue great questions of constitutional law in the editorial columns of the Gazette. The depth, the fine discrimination, the iron-linked logic of those disquisitions, were surpassed by nothing I heard from the first lawyers of the land while on the Supreme Bench."

Mr. Edward D. Mansfield said that he knew of no writer who could express an idea so clearly and so briefly. "He wrote the pure old English—the vernacular tongue, unmixed with French or Latin phrases or idioms, and unperverted with any scholastic logic. His language was like himself—plain, sensible, and unaffected. His force, however, lay not so much in this as in his truth, honesty, and courage, those moral qualities which made him distinguished at that day, and would distinguish him now."

The Revolutionary War left George Hammond poor, and hoping to better his condition, he removed with his family and slaves to Western Virginia, in 1785, locating near Wellsburg, in Brooke county.

Judge Cranmer, of the Wheeling Bar, says that "he was a man of education and some culture, and possessed a retentive memory and an appreciative taste. He would frequently recite whole plays of Shakespeare, and he had committed to memory Young's Night Thoughts, and many other poems. He was a man of uncommon mental force and physical endurance. He was tall and spare; his carriage was erect and imposing. He had firm, practical judgment, uncompromising prejudices, was a thoughtful reader, and a good talker."

A picture of no common man.

Charles Hammond inclined to the printing business, but finding no encouragement in Washington, whither he had gone, he returned to the West, and in 1800 entered the law office of Philip Doddridge, a name not without honor in the Old Dominion. Hammond was admitted to practice in the state courts and the courts of the United States, in 1803. In the first year of his graduation as an attorney, he married Sarah Tillinghast, and settled in Wheeling.

Something of the intellectual grasp that so greatly distinguished Alexander Hamilton was also characteristic of the mind of Charles Hammond; not in as high degree, perhaps, but still in a high degree. Within a year after his admission to the Bar, and when only twenty-four years of age, Hammond was employed in a case arising under the excise law, and made an argument on the constitutional questions involved that attracted very wide attention. It was issued in the East and accepted by the Federalists as sound in doctrine. The editor of the United States Gazette, who printed it entire to the exclusion of much other matter, said that the importance of the questions discussed and the ability displayed were sufficient apology to his readers for giving so much space to it.

I pass directly to a celebrated case, in which Hammond and Clay were pitted against each other, merely noting chronologically that it was in 1810 that Hammond removed to Ohio and settled on a farm near St. Clairsville; that a year later, he began the publication of the Ohio Federalist, which he continued until 1818; that the exigencies of the Federalist party, of which he was the leader, required him, in 1813, to stand for the State Senate, to which he was elected; that at the request of the Bar, he served as a member of the House for five years, refusing, in 1821, to spend further time; that he made a revision of the laws of Ohio, and was the author of the acts regulating the course of descents, distribution of personal estates, and chancery proceedings; and that he accepted the appointment of Reporter for the Court in Bank, and edited the first ten volumes of Ohio Reports. During all these years, he was exceedingly busy in the practice, the interests of his clients often calling him to Washington.

The melancholy failure of Mr. Madison's administration, and the financial distress logically resulting from embargoes and unsound theories inherited from the Jefferson administration, unwise relations between the national treasury and state banks and overtrading on every hand, compelled the establishment of a new United States Bank in 1816. Mr. Calhoun reported the bill, and led the debate in favor of the measure in speeches that contrast strangely with his nullifying arguments sixteen years later. Mr. Madison signed the bill with great reluctance. When in operation, the Bank established branches in different cities, and, among other places, at Cincinnati and Chillicothe, Ohio. The people of the Ohio and Mississippi Valleys were largely indebted for land, and, instead of finding relief through these banking agencies, their embarrassments became so onerous as to lead them to cast about for some agency of relief more closely allied to their interests than the eastern corporation. They saw, or fancied they saw, the little specie in the Mississippi Valley fast disappearing over the mountains and the ruin of the business newly begun since the close of the war. Hence, the anti-bank movement in Ohio. Here, parties were changed in their relations to the institution. The Jeffersonians who had denounced the old United States Bank were the supporters of the new United States Bank, and the Federalists were the leaders in the opposition, although all parties shared in the feeling of discontent.

In 1819, Ohio passed a general act, taxing banks, individuals, and companies transacting a banking business in the state without being authorized to do so by the laws thereof, and providing that if the United States Bank should continue to transact business in the state after the 15th September ensuing, it should pay a tax of $50,000 for each branch, and made it mandatory on the Auditor of State to assess and collect the tax. Ralph Osborn was Auditor, and on the day assigned, his agent, John L. Harper, assisted by Thomas Orr, appeared at the Chillicothe Bank just as the cashier was opening the safe and forcibly took possession of $100,-000 in coin and bank notes, which they bore off to Columbus and deposited with H. M. Curry, Treasurer of the State. Curry, upon retiring from office, delivered this money to his successor, Mr. Sullivan, and informed him that it was the money collected from the United States Bank. It was kept separate and apart from the State deposits, in obedience to an injunction granted by the United States Circuit Court. These are the names that figure as appellants in the celebrated case of Osborn v. The Bank of the United States. There was intense excitement throughout the Union at this forcible entry of the bank by officers of the state. In view of the decision of the Supreme Court in McCulloch v. The State of Maryland, the bold act seemed like defiance of national authority. The Bank employed Henry Clay as attorney, and the state Charles Hammond. Harper and Orr went to jail, where they remained for many months, refusing the bail the Bank pressed upon them. Details of the legal fencing in this case would be interesting had we time. When a decision was reached in the Circuit Court, in 1821, Hammond appealed the case to the Supreme Court of the United States. Pending final hearing, there was great activity in the public prints, among legal pamphleteers. The Ohio Legislature published an appeal to the people (written by Hammond), copies of which were sent to Jefferson and Madison and drew forth guarded compliments from these retired statesmen. The Governor and General Assembly of Connecticut and the Legislatures of New Hampshire and New York had something to say upon the contest. Virginia and Georgia had cases of their own, and an effort was made to combine the influence of these with Ohio so as to make the opposition to the Bank side more formidable. Expectation in the West already contemplated a victory. Governor Brown declared that, in his opinion, the Ohio pamphlet reviewing the decision of the court in McCulloch v. Maryland so completely refuted the Supreme Court

2

that, as the judges were not deficient in intelligence, they could not fail to feel much chagrin. The management of the Bank was very exasperating. "The mammoth Bank," says Hammond to Wright, December 14, "has been taking more rash measures. It has required the poor devils at Cincinnati to renew their notes and pay the reductions and discounts at Chillicothe. They have demurred, and yesterday *precipes* came to the Clerk of the Federal Court, putting the whole debts in suit—about one hundred. Gen. Harrison's heart began to misgive him for uniting in my report to put them out of the protection of state laws. These *precipes* come opportunely to brace his resolution."

The question was, what would the great Chief Justice do? Would he permit a review of McCulloch *v.* Maryland? To solve the doubt, Hammond, in 1823, wrote an argument, which he submitted to Marshall, accompanied by a letter, in which the wishes of the anti-bank party were frankly expressed. The response is not without interest to us:

MARSHALL TO HAMMOND.

RICHMOND, *December* 28, 1823.

DEAR SIR:

I received some time past your printed argument in the case of Sullivan and others against the Bank of the United States, and, a day or two afterwards, your letter of the 4th instant which was intended to accompany it. I have read the argument with that pleasure which I always feel in reading or hearing one in which the subject is discussed with real ability, whether I concur or not in opinion with the person who makes it. This is certainly exempt from any thing like the charge of Jacobinism or disrespect to the court, and is at the same time, I think, less vulnerable than a certain re- port* to which you allude, which, however, was far from being deficient in vigor.

If Judge Washington will not consent to receive it absolutely and unconditionally as an argument, it must be read over in court, and he must view it in the light of notes, and as a substitute for those which might be taken by himself.

I abstain scrupulously from all intermeddling in the election of President; but as your letter on that sub- ject was undoubtedly intended to be seen, I have shown it to some gentlemen who will not fail to communicate its contents to others. A resolution is now before our House of Delegates recommending a congressional caucus. It may probably pass; but not without some considerable opposition. It is supported by the friends of Mr. Crawford, who undoubtedly constitute a ma- jority of the assembly, and I believe of the state. I rather conjecture that Mr. Clay is the second man with Virginia. I, however, know too little of public opin- ion to say any thing about it which deserves attention. For myself I can say that I consider Mr. Clay as an enlighted statesman who has ever since his mission to Europe acted on a system which displays enlarged and liberal views; and I think him entitled to particular credit for having brought the Missouri conflict to a

---

* Doubtless the report to the Ohio Legislature written by Ham- mond.

peaceful termination. I shall be perfectly content with the choice of the nation, whoever he may be.

With great respect and esteem, I am, sir, your obedient   J. MARSHALL.

This argument was finally made before the court in February, 1824. It was a master-piece. Admirable in temper, perfect in logical construction, comprehensive in its grasp of principles, original, and as a specimen of English composition, will challenge comparison with any thing emanating from the most eminent of the legal profession. Hammond's reputation was already great, but this increased it although the decision of the Supreme Court was against him. To attempt to give you a clear idea of the argument, would be to mar a work that should be considered as a whole to be enjoyed and appreciated.

Mr. Edward D. Mansfield in his Memoirs says, that Hammond in his argument advocated States Rights, an error inexcusable in so industrious a writer. Mr. Hammond was a Nationalist of the Washington school, and in this Bank case he was careful to leave no doubt of his position. He was endeavoring to ascertain the liabilities of states—their constitutional limitations, as well as to have determined the extent of the jurisdiction of the Circuit Courts. He laid down the proposition that the State of Ohio was the sole defendant in this cause, and by the eleventh amendment of the Constitution of the United States, the Circuit Court was excluded—that it was a case of original jurisdiction in which the Supreme Court alone was authorized to act. This proposition is enforced with a clearness of explication and force of reasoning that seems to leave no opening for further discussion. " The question whether the Bank of the United States," said Mr. Hammond, "as now constituted, is exempt by the Constitution of the Union from the taxing power of the state, depends upon the nature and character of the institution. If it stands upon the same foundation with the mint and post-office—if its business can justly be assimilated to the process and proceedings of the federal courts, I admit without hesitation that it is entitled to the exemption it claims. The states can not tax the offices, establishments, and operations of the national government. It is not the argument of the opinion in Maryland and McCulloch, but the premises upon which that argument is founded, that I ask the court now to re-examine and re-consider. I ask what that opinion, as I conceive, does not contain—a full, distinct, and explicit exposition and definiton of the true nature and character of the Bank."

" Whether Congress could constitutionally create a Bank, was not and ought not to have been considered an open question in 1819. It was certainly injudicious to move this question, and connect it with that of exemption from taxation by the states, when they stand wholly unconnected. The power to incorporate a Bank is one thing, the privileges with which it may be invested is another, and a very different thing. The old Bank established in 1791, preserved faithfully the character given to it by its founders ; it answered all the purposes, and effected all the advantages anticipated by its friends, and terminated its existence without producing any of the mischief predicted by its enemies.

It originated, existed, and acted in the true spirit of the Constitution ; and of necessity, good, and not evil was the result."

The original founders of the first Bank of the United States did not claim for it immunity from taxation, as incident to its charter. Nor did the politicians or jurists of the time consider it as entitled to any privilege of the kind. It was taxed by the State of Georgia; the tax was collected and kept. The opinion of the court in the case of *Deveaux* seemed obviously to recognize the power of taxation. It treated the Bank as a company of traders, not as a public institution.

The second Bank of the United States—the Bank of 1816—was established under different circumstances, and by different hands. It was established by those who once represented an incorporation as some " great, independent, substantial thing ; as a political end of peculiar magnitude and moment." And although the attempt to fasten this character upon it, was made, for the purpose of proving it an alien to the Constitution, yet, in perfect consistency with their original opinions, they claimed for the institution in their hands, that very character, so earnestly disclaimed by the original advocates of the power to incorporate. They were not content to derive quality and capacity from their charter. They claimed political power and political exemption.

The corollary resulting from Mr. Hammond's reasoning was, that the creation of a corportion did not confer political power or political character, and that the operations, as well as the property of the Bank, were subject to the same rule of taxation as the operations and property of other associations. The Bank, notwithstanding their charter, remained a private association, bound by a contract for a consideration paid, to perform certain employments for the government. To decide that the Bank was a public instrument standing in the same relation to the government as a public office and its incumbent, would necessarily involve the government in some strange and monstrous practices. The very fact that the stockholders paid a consideration in money for their chartered privileges, forbade attaching to their public employments the character of a public office.

"Let the doctrine be established," said he, "that the states can not tax either the institutions, or the property of the nation, and that Congress can withdraw nothing that is private from the taxing power of the states, and the division line is clearly and distinctly marked."

"It derogates nothing from the supremacy of the national government to assert that private property neither exists nor is introduced by its authority. Its objects are national, not municipal. If it creates private property by a grant of lands, its power over the land ceases when the grant is completed; its subsequent disposition and protection appertains to the states. If it grant a patent for useful inventions, it is in virtue of a specific power, and the invention when brought into use becomes subject to state legislation. So if it grant a corporate franchise to individuals to conduct a private trade, it confers a capacity, but can not regulate the business. It may provide for the naturalization of aliens, but it can not authorize aliens to acquire or hold estates. In all these cases, the act done by the national government is supreme, so far as its power extends."

Mr. Hammond concluded as follows: " The proposition I have labored to sustain, is plain, precise, and unambiguous. It is, that whatever is private property is subject to the taxing power of the states; that whatever is private business and employment, is subject to the same power, excepting a tax on exports, imports and tonnage. This proposition is founded upon the express letter of the Constitution, and in its very terms excludes all pretension to tax the offices, institutions, or property of the national government. If this power of assessing taxes be confined to the private individual property found or employed within the territorial limits of the state, its exercise never can become repugnant to the constitutional laws of the Union. If a law of the Union be enacted, which assumes to restrain the exercise of this power upon the ground of repugnancy, such law can not be warranted by the Constitution. For the Constitution can not, at the same time, authorize an exercise of power by the states and a restraint of that power by the nation.

" This proposition, so simple in its terms, so easy to be understood, so free from all complexity or difficulty in its application, is neither denied nor admitted. But an attempt is made to escape its consequences by advancing other propositions, and deducing corrollaries, by which the question is instantly involved in confusion, from which the most highly-gifted powers of argument have failed to extricate it.

"It has ever appeared to me that the error of the argument I have endeavored to confute, consists in two misconceptions of the case—first, in considering the Bank, as an institution of the government, of a strictly public character ; and, secondly, in regarding the power of taxation claimed for the states as extending to every description of property and business, national as well as individual, public as well as private. It has been my object to remove these misconceptions and place the subject before the court in what I have considered its true light—the Bank, as an association of individuals, conducting a private trade for their own advantage and emolument ; the right of taxation as extending to nothing but the property and business of private individuals. When thus considered, I have attempted to demonstrate that the power to tax is not repugnant to the power to create or preserve, and can not be drawn into collision with any legitimate power of the national government.

"I have founded no argument upon a supposed abuse of power by Congress. I have sought to reconcile no inconsistencies by '*the magic of the word* CONFIDENCE.' In governments constituted like ours, such topics of argument are, at best, of little force. If the national government may abuse power, so may the states ; if the states may call for confidence, so may the national government. Where power is conferred, confidence is reposed that it will be executed for the public good. Where power is denied, the public good can not justify an attempt to exercise it. If the Constitution leaves, in the hands of the states, power by which they may do mischief, this court can not deprive them of it. If the action of the national government be imperfect in consequence of a defect of power, this court can not help it. The Constitution itself is the rule. To that we must resort; and we must determine the extent of its provisions by the known and established maxims of interpretation. It has declared the cases in which the states shall not exercise the power of taxation. The effect of this declaration is, that they can not be restrained in the exercise of this power in any cases but those specified. Every attempt to withdraw individual property from the action of this power, in other cases, is an attempt to do that which the people in their sovereign capacity alone can do—to change the principles of the Constitution."

The point raised by Mr. Hammond as to jurisdiction moved the court to ask for a reargument, and the Bank hastened to bring in Daniel Webster and John Sergeant to assist Mr. Clay. It is not known how the court was divided originally on the question of jurisdiction, but after the reargument Justice Johnston only dissented.

"The full pressure of this argument is felt," said the great Chief Justice, "and the difficulties it presents are acknowledged. The direct interest of the state in the suit, as brought, is admitted; and had it been in the power of the Bank to make it a party, perhaps no decree ought to have been pronounced in the cause, until the state was before the court. But this was not in the power of the Bank. The eleventh amendment of the

Constitution has exempted a state from the suits of citizens of other states, or aliens; and the very difficult question is to be decided, whether in such a case the court may act upon the agents employed by the state, and on the property in their hands."

And then, before proceeding with his argument, he indulges in a patriotic exordium, which, in the light of more recent history, has a striking, a pathetic interest to us.

The great Virginian is at his best. In pertinence of illustration, in vigor and in subtlety of reasoning, perhaps no other one of his remarkable opinions surpasses this. He boldly asserts the public character of the Bank, and at a stroke evades the dilemma presented by Hammond, and rescues the opinion in the case of McCulloch v. Maryland, thus opening the Circuit Courts to the Bank of the United States without limitation. The patriotic impulse carried him beyond the logical line of his argument, into the realm of partisanship. The determination to strengthen the Bank by bringing to its support in all cases the protection of the Federal Courts is apparent. As a political policy, this was unwise. The anti-bank party leaders were not slow to seize upon the advantage thus given to them and to stimulate popular prejudices against the consolidation of political power with wealth. Upon this wave, Andrew Jackson and the modern Democratic party rode into power.

There is one point in that decision which has an important bearing on a question of living interest, viz: the relations of the national government to corporations. Marshall said:

" That the mere business of banking is, in its own

nature, a private business, and may be carried on by individuals or companies having no political connection with the government, is admitted; but the Bank is not such an individual or company. It was not created for its own sake, or for private purposes. *It has never been supposed that Congress could create such a corporation.*" You mark the passage. Has Congress, as this language of the greatest expounder of the Constitution implies, chartered railroad and other companies without due authority?

We have had a glimpse, and I fear a very imperfect and unsatisfactory one, of Charles Hammond as a jurist.

Before dismissing this part of our subject, it will be interesting to know something of Chief Justice Marshall's opinion of Hammond. The compliment paid in the letter I read and in the decision of the court, was repeated a few months later in a private conversation, and being free from all official formality, is more interesting to us.

Lieut. Governor Greene, of Rhode Island, relates that in 1824, after the conclusion of the great Bank case, he took a trip with Chief Justice Marshall down the Potomac, and the latter made many inquiries about Hammond. "He spoke of his remarkable acuteness and accuracy of mind, and referred with emphatic admiration to his argument before the Supreme Court in the Bank case. He said that he had met no judicial record of equal intellectual power since Lord Hardwick's time."

Governor Greene, who knew Hammond intimately during the last twenty years of his life, and himself was prominent as a lawyer, expressed the opinion publicly after Hammond's decease that, "intellectually he was without a superior in our country."

"In the legal action of his mind, he was eminently self-reliant, and cared little for what is called authority, except as it agreed with his own views. In this respect, he belonged to the same class as the English Holt, Hardwick, and Mansfield, and the American Marshall, Parsons, and Webster. These men got their law from their own minds, and not mainly from books that recorded the opinions of others; in other words they made authority rather than followed it."

So much for Hammond's career at the Bar.

Personally, I have a deeper interest in him as a journalist and popular advocate of principles dear to mankind, and we shall now consider his work in this field. Charles Hammond was the most distinguished American editor of his day. In one respect, he has never been equaled. In a consistent adherence to principle, through a long series of years of professional labor. On this account quite as much as on account of great ability, is to be attributed the extent and endurance of his influence. Many a young journalist since his day has found the shadow of this traditional fame following him in all his efforts, and while crushed by the inevitable comparison he has been nerved to greater effort. Yet journalism to Hammond was an incident merely in his career. He was by intellectual endowments, education, temperament, and taste, fitted for the bar. He said that he added journalism to eke out an income sufficient for his family. It is true that until he reached the age of forty-five he was poor; but I suspect that writing was essential to his complete intellectual enjoyment. He had a message to deliver to the world, if you please, an irresistible impulse to be useful to society. The newspaper was the means. Mr. Hammond was a man of strong political convictions, but a pure and lofty patriotism was the guiding principle

George Hammond was a slaveholder, and it is believed that a repugnance to the system is what induced Charles to cross the river into Ohio, in 1810. He never failed to speak plainly of it on all appropriate occasions. A newspaper was the medium through which he could most effectually reach the public conscience. The political principles which he had espoused, were being trampled in the dust, and he seized the opportunity to enter the arena, and bid defiance to all comers. He established the *Ohio Federalist*, at St. Clairsville, and became the leader of the party in the state. The weight of his opposition was felt. Embargo laws and war with England, were themes treated by him with greater wit and sarcasm than was displayed by "A New England Farmer."

We learn something of this Federalist in the Personal Recollections which that sterling citizen, Robert Buchanan left. He says:

"My first aquaintance with Mr. Hammond was about 1813, through his paper the *Ohio Federalist*, then published at St. Clairsville. I had met with it casually, and noticing some pungent and witty articles against the war then in full blast, and Mr. Clay, who in after years was his bosom friend, I subscribed for it—weekly $3.50 per annum.

"It was against my politics, for like all boys, I

was for the present and next war, careless of consequences, and Mr. Clay, being then a strong advocate of the war in Congress, was a great favorite. But I loved fun, and in Mr. Hammond's articles that was to be found."

The publication of the *Federalist* ceased in 1818, and Hammond, with all the rest of the Federalists, was absorbed by the Republican party, under the influence of the Monroe administration. But he was no less a Washington Federalist than before, for twenty years later we find him saying: "It is, it has been my pride to follow in the paths where they (Washington, Hamilton, and Jay) led, *longum intervallum*, indeed, but with unshaken confidence and unfaltering step."

All questions of interest to the American people were discussed by him during these years of activity at the Bar, including the question of slavery. Of these, his earlier utterances, I shall make no mention, as prior to the Missouri controversy, the shadow over the Union was but as the breadth of one's hand.

He influenced the Legislature of Ohio, in 1819, to adopt his views, and to declare that the existence of slavery had ever been deemed a great moral and political evil; that its tendency was to impair our national character and materially affect our national happiness; and that inasmuch as the extension of a slave population in the United States was fraught with the most fearful consequences to the permanency and durability of our Republican institutions, therefore it should be strenuously resisted, and the Senators of that state in Congress were instructed accordingly.

Later, in his correspondence in 1820, he flamed out

against this proposed extension of slavery: " I am filled with wrath," said he to John C. Wright, "at the trick put upon the yankees in the Senate plan to bring in Maine. Let Maine go to the devil (the state, a legal entity now-a-days) rather than make a state of it in concession to the slave interest.

" The Slave States move in a compact body. Others are disturbed by constitutional scruples. I am in hopes the states where there are no slaves, can in due season find men who do not bogle upon that point. That is, in my mind, a great question, and fraught with important consequences. A new state of parties must grow out of it. Give me a Northern President, whether John Quincy Adams or DeWitt Clinton, or anybody else, rather than that things should remain as they are."

The depth of Mr. Hammond's hatred of slavery, with which he was associated in his youth, is shown in this proposition to make Mr. Adams the candidate, toward whom he felt a prejudice on account of what he believed to be his apostacy from Federalism during Mr. Jefferson's administration. He would condone this grave political sin to advance the cause of freedom.

The West resolved to stand by Mr. Clay, and under the leadership of Mr. Hammond, the contest was fought out with great vigor. His plan was to have Mr. Clay first nominated by the Legislature of Ohio, and then to combine the States of Ohio, Indiana, Illinois, and Kentucky in his support. To further this plan he wrote a pamphlet as early as 1822, which was widely circulated.

In 1823, Hammond opened the campaign formally

in the Gazette, in an able discussion of men and measures which would engage the attention of the American people. He foresaw that the election would be carried into the House. The important measures, internal improvements and domestic manufactures, were to be the test of political wisdom, and govern the ultimate choice. "To make effective these principles of public policy," said Hammond, "involving the manifest interests of the nation, we want no military man at the head of our affairs, but, on the contrary, a statesman, well versed in the science of government, a man of moderation, yet firm and resolute, and possessed of a steady but pacific temperament. Such a man, if we have been rightly informed, is not General Jackson. He is impatient and impetuous, and loves the noise and din of the camp more than the peaceful labors of the cabinet."

But while thus conducting Mr. Clay's campaign—what is more correctly the Clay-Adams campaign—he did not cease to strike heavy blows at slavery. The supporters of the system had become aggressive. The success in the case of Missouri incited them to seek new territory for their property. Thus, Dr. Floyd, of Virginia, had used this language in an address to his constituents : "The grand objection to Mr. Adams is his having ceded to Spain the province of Texas, a territory which would have made two Slave-holding States, and secured to the Southern interest four Senators."

"Such language," said Mr. Hammond, "is too plain to be misapprehended, and coming from a member of Congress, discovers the views and feelings which will prevail among the slave-holding members on every important national question. A coalition, cemented by a sameness of manners, and by a mutuality of interests, will be formed, and when once it can get the predominance, will overpower and trample under foot all opposition. We can not help making the inquiry whether such views are not opposed to the prosperity and peace of the United States? And whether men who wish an extension of slavery for political purposes, are not advocating measures which lead not only to moral degradation and misery, but to great ultimate national calamities. To urge the farther extention of involuntary servitude, appears, not only morally wrong, but politically dangerous." Words of wisdom, but alas! unheeded by government or people then. In time all became conscious of their sagacity. Men individually rarely, and organized into communities never, at first choose as the Corinthian hero of old—

"Life or death,
But never death in life for me, O King."

The campaign which began in 1824, having for its ultimate object the possession of political power, and the distribution of the spoils, was the most remarkable in many respects in the history of our government—remarkable in its violence of conduct and abuse of men, and in the fact that a political party depended entirely upon greed, ignorance, prejudice, and passion, for success. It would have succeeded in 1824, but for a single circumstance, viz: the financial distress of the country, which compelled attention to business interests. The value of property had fallen 50 per cent in ten years. The balance of trade being largely against us, the country was drained of its specie, and there was embarrassment in all of the centers of trade, and distress every-where. The protective policy was extorted from unwilling public men, whose favorite theory did not admit of its necessity to an agricultural and commercial people. The result was the election of Adams through the help of Clay, and the postponement of the Jackson-Democratic spoils era for four years.

During the contest, Hammond, in a pamphlet formulated the platform for the Adams-Clay party. It was *Protection to American Industry, and Internal Improve-ments.* What came after in Whig days, was but a repetition of this in more elaborate phrase, suited to the growing importance of Mr. Clay's American system. An attempt was made to compel Jackson to show his hand on the tariff, but that old fox was quietly making terms with Pennsylvania, before the vote of Tennessee was recorded. "How is it," wrote Hammond to Clay, "that no one speaks freely of this man? Is he not acting the part of a most contemptible seeker after popularity? Instead of being a frank, open, fearless, honest man, is he not the victim of strong passions and prejudices, violent when irresponsible, cautious when differently situated, ambitious, vain and hasty, a fit instrument for others to work upon, subject to be governed by flatterers, and still inclined to hate every man of talents who has firmness to look through him, and speak of him as he deserves? I think he is strongly endowed with these traits of character, and that if classed as a mere animal, he would be a kind of monkey-tiger. I do not know but that it would be well for such a monster to be placed in the Presidential chair for the

next term.   King Snake succeeding King Log, and the
citizen frogs made to scamper.   I am almost sure that if
I had been this winter at Washington, I should have
contrived to quarrel with him.   I dislike him for cause,
I hate him peremptorily, and I could wish that his supporters for the presidency, one and all were snugly by
themselves in some Island of Barrataria, and he be their
King, provided, that they constituted the entire population.   They would make a glorious terrestrial pande-
monium, and as fast as they cut each other's throats the
world would be rid of very troublesome politicians, and,
in general, right worthless citizens."   But instead of an
island, we know that His Majesty, in 1829, took possession of the continent, and punished his enemies in
right royal style; and that he set such an example of
lust for power as to move almost the entire population
of these United States to emulate it; every boy carry-
ing pinned in his hat this legend: The highest prize is
possible to every American.

But to return to Mr. Clay's campaign of 1824:
During the campaign, Hammond was urged from
Washington to undertake to form a union between Mr.
Crawford and Mr. Clay, but he declined to be the agent.
Mr. Clay, in a confidential letter from Frankfort, Oc-
tober 25th, said: "You treated the proposition from
the friends of Mr. Crawford in regard to the Vice-Presidency, transmitted to you, with much discretion and
propriety. . . . It was impossible to accede to it,
and it was impracticable if it had been accepted. As
for me, before I could listen to it, I must entirely
change my nature and character and violate all the principles which I have made my guide during the agitation

of the Presidential question. According to these principles, I have felt it my duty to abstain from every species of compromitment; to reject every overture looking to arrangements or compromises; and to preserve my perfect freedom of action, whether I am elected or not.

. . . "Of one thing you and the rest of my friends may be perfectly assured, that if I am elected, I shall enter upon the office without one solitary promise or pledge to any man to redeem; and if I am not elected, I will at least preserve unsullied that public integrity and those principles which my friends have supposed me to possess.

"What course my friends may take, what it may be proper for me to pursue in the event of my not entering the House of Representatives, I have not yet determined. I have indeed purposely postponed the consideration of that question, partly from a hope that it may not be necessary to decide it, and partly from the embarrassments incident to it.

"There are strong objections to each of the three gentlemen from among whom we may have to make a selection. How can we get over in regard to Mr. Crawford:

"1. The caucus nomination by a *minority*.

"2. The state of his health.

"3. The principles of administration which there is reason to fear will be adopted by him from his position and his Southern support?"

Mr. Clay had sanguine expectations of the West. He said he might lose one vote in Illinois, but the rest would undoubtedly stand by him. If New York should vote for either Mr. Adams or Mr. Crawford he did not despair of Virginia.

This letter has a historic value, as we shall see later when we come to consider the charges of bargain and sale.

As to what should be Mr. Clay's policy if defeated, Mr. Hammond advised that he should retain the office of Speaker of the House, as in no subordinate position could he be so useful. It was the chiefest blunder of his career that Mr. Clay failed to heed this advice of his friend. But ambition knows no halting place short of the possession of power. If it can not possess the throne, it must possess the power behind the throne. The office of Secretary of State was supposed to be the place of power. From that office, Presidents had stepped into the White House for a quarter of a century.

The Jackson leaders were determined that Mr. Clay should not take that step. When they failed to make a bargain—for a bargain they attempted—with Clay, they opened a war of slander—slander the most vile that disappointment could invent. They charged bargain and sale against Adams and Clay, and invented testimony to sustain the charge. Out of their own evil hearts, they judged these two. There is abundant evidence accessible now to prove this. Mr. Clay, justly indignant at the personal assaults, unwisely took notice of his detractors, and in a public card denounced the Pennsylvanian who circulated the slander as "an infamous caluminator, a dastard, and liar." Very true words, but Mr. Clay should have been superior to their utterance. Hammond saw the mistake. To a correspondent, he wrote under date of February 10th : " I am concerned at Clay's card. He is out of temper. He calls hard names. He lets himself down to the level of Printers' Devils, which things ought not to be. But we are not all wise at all times. There are some poor devils in the Pennsylvania delegation who are beneath his level, and his publication will not bring them out—and if it does, where's the honor? and if it does not, who is disgraced? I regret the publication, and have no more to say."

When Clay's nomination came before the Senate for confirmation, Branch, of North Carolina, made a violent speech against it; and all of the Jackson men, and some of Crawford's friends, voted against confirmation. Revenge did not control all, as we learn from a letter from General Harrison to Hammond, dated March 9th, 1825, that " Mason told Rowan and myself yesterday that his vote against Clay was not on account of his conduct on the election of President, but for his construction of the Constitution, I suppose, in relation to internal improvements."

You have in this the real reason for the alliance between Adams and Clay : it was one of principle. They both favored protection to American industry and governmental aid to internal improvements. It was on that platform that the campaign was conducted by the friends of Mr. Clay, as we have seen ; and Mr. Adams was the only one of the three entering the House who sympathized with this policy. For Mr. Clay to have cast his vote for either Crawford or Jackson would have been to sacrifice his principles and his friends. We have seen what he said in his letter to Hammond about the extreme Southern views of Crawford which he could not approve. Not only did this objection lie against Jackson, but there was also a personal antagonism of long standing. Why did not intelligent men accept these rational and natural reasons for Mr. Clay's course? Because party necessity required a campaign of detraction and misrepresentation to render nugatory the measures of the new administration, so strong in capacity, and the elements of usefulness.

Hammond struck such vigorous blows upon the enemy as to receive compliments from Peter Force and a warm letter of thanks from Clay.

The campaign of slander was prosecuted with constantly augmenting violence during the Adams administration. The conspirators had succeeded so well in poisoning the public mind by 1826 as to foreshadow their success in 1828. The opposition was consolidated. "There is a terrible feeling of rancor," wrote Hammond, "infused into the public mind against Clay. The union of Crawford, Calhoun, Jackson, and Clinton to attack him is rather unexpected. They have at least that point of cohesion—deadly enmity—which their united strength can alone gratify. It is perhaps as strong as any other—at least, for the purpose of destruction."

During the contest the Crawford business was brought forward to prove Clay's corruption. As Hammond represented Clay, upon receipt of a letter from his friend, he came forward with a clear, manly statement addressed to Gales and Seaton, but it was refused admittance to the columns of the Intelligencer. If a newspaper of to-day were to refuse such an act of justice towards a man of Mr. Clay's prominence, it would dig its own grave.

John Randolph, of Roanoke, whom it would be charity to suppose mad, was put forward to lead the opposition in Congress. The speeches on the Panama Mission were designed to consolidate the slaveholders against the administration. The shocking black-guardism which characterizes them, was merely incidental. "I should suppose," said Hammond, "that the cloven foot of negro slavery and Southern dominancy is so manifest in the votes connected with Randolph's speeches, that some of our free state Jacksonians must open their eyes." He improved the opportunity to discuss the question of slavery in a series of brilliant editorials in the Gazette, which created a profound impression. His argument hewed to the constitutional line, and the rights of all under the fundamental law were clearly defined. To Hayne's appeal to the House, "Let us then cease to talk of slavery; let us cease to negotiate upon any subject connected with it," Hammond replied, pointing out the absurdity of such a proposition, which was made within three years of the adoption of a resolution requesting the President to prosecute negotiations with the maritime powers for the effectual abolition of the slave trade. Hammond's argument was on the clauses of the Constitution bearing on slavery, apportionment, representation, the protection of states against domestic violence, etc.

The power to regulate commerce among the several states, is given to Congress. Traffic in slaves was one species of commerce, and was therefore subject to the regulations of the national government. The power of prohibiting this commerce altogether, and to confine the slaves to their habitations in the slave states, was necessarily involved in this provision. The right to property in slaves, he said, could not be questioned by the Federal Government, or by any state beyond its own territory. But in every thing else, slaves and slavery, like other persons, property, and things, were subjects, and proper subjects of legislation and negotiations, not to be slightly interfered with, but when a proper case should arise, to be acted upon calmly, decisively, and fearlessly, regardless of the blustering of interested denunciation. "*Fiat justitia, ruat coelum.*"

Randolph, he styled the Senatorial Thersites, and proved that he filched from Burke in the oratory which the faithful deemed matchless. With the skill of a master in Hudabrastic work, he drew from the Iliad a striking portrait of the man of Roanoke, whose sharp voice pierced the ears of his auditor in shrillest tone.

> " Loquacious, loud and turbulent of tongue :
> Awed by no shame by no respect controlled ;
> In scandal busy, in reproach bold ;
> Scorn all his joy, and laughter all his aim ;
> But chief he gloried with licentious style,
> To lash the great, and statesmen to revile.
> His figure such as might his soul proclaim.
>
> . . . . .
>
> Spleen to mankind his envious soul possest,
> And much hated all, but most the best."

One fact will explain the anomalous condition of things during these days of party strife. Mr. Adams's Postmaster-General was a Jackson man, and participated in the warfare upon the President and his Secretary of

State. Such a lack of the sense of honor in a man who afterwards held a position on the Supreme Bench, and aspired to the highest place seems almost inexplicable. His own correspondence which I have seen, makes it a clear case of disingenuousness. In a letter, April 19, 1826, from Mr. Clay to Mr. Hammond, I find the following statement:

"As to the association of our names, I have seen nothing to wound me. I am provoked with a little article smuggled into the National Intelligencer under the editorial head (I understand by the Postmaster-General) casting an indecent reflection on you, as the assumed author of a certain letter."

And then he refers to a delicate subject I suspect much nearer his heart:

"The Panama articles in the Liberty Hall are able and highly useful. The remarks on slavery are fully justified by the course of Mr. Randolph, etc., still it is a subject on which there should be mutual forbearance, and perhaps most on the side of the non-slaveholding states, as the stronger, safer, and happier party." Thirteen years later, when Henry Clay himself was constrained to appear in the Senate as the defender of the institution of Slavery, Hammond reminded him of this letter approving his editorial on the Panama Mission, which was written when he was in the vigor of a noble manhood.

I must pass by Mr. Clay's affair of honor with Randolph, and his correspondence with Hammond in which much interesting history of a personal character is to be found. Clay said that he was compelled to send the challenge; that he rejoiced that no injury had happened to Randolph; and that he regretted only that the religious and moral part of the community would feel offended. Submission longer on his part would have rendered existence intolerable.

The din of personal warfare did not prevent the friends from indulging in much pleasant confidential correspondence on the political outlook. Clay was disappointed in the result of the Illinois election, but his optimistic mind drew comfort and hope from Maryland, New Jersey, and Pennsylvania. *"Fas est doceri ab hoste"*—it is proper to take counsel from one's enemy—wrote Hammond, and he expressed the hope that Mr. Adams would disappoint Tazewell & Co., by leaving no vulnerable point of attack in his message. The message is to Hammond's taste, brief, statemanlike, and written in a style that may very well serve as a model to Presidents.

These days of hope and sunshine are but for a season. The war of detraction, of villiany, goes on more vigorously than ever. In a little over a year the political sky is overcast with thunderous clouds. Hammond instituted a libel suit in his own defense, and advised Clay "to accept the defiance of his enemies and ask of the House an investigation of the charges against him."

Clay lost the control of his own state, and in despair Hammond gave him up for 1828. He suggested that it might be well to hint to Virginia to break down the new Democracy by bringing father Monroe once more to the front. But it was .decided all round that Mr. Adams should be supported as against Jackson. This decision was reached with great reluctance. Why? The answer will be found to be instructive to us. The administration of Mr. Adams must stand in our history

as one of the purest and ablest since the foundation of
the government. It was devoted to the fostering of the
industrial interests and the direction of public affairs on
strict business principles. It stands out as the one non-
partisan administration. It had not a trace of color
in it. And here was the trouble. There was nothing
for the boys to rally round. The business people, gen-
erally, were for the re-election of Mr. Adams. He had
influenced the adoption of wise financial and commercial
measures, and the golden music of a sound currency
was heard in the land once more. But there was nothing for ambition to lay hold of. Nobody was turned
out of office except for cause, and death seldom entered
the Federal temples. Hammond had to protest most
vigorously against the threatened appointment of John
McLean (the Jackson Postmaster-General) to fill a va-
cancy in the Circuit Court. He said to his friend, " I
shall consider the appointment of McLean as an indis-
cretion, evincing such incorrect views, or such incapacity
of judgment as makes it clear that the administration
can not sustain itself. No administration ever did, no
one ever can succeed, that proceeds upon the ground of
conciliating open or covert hostility. Such conduct is
the result of fear, of a total want of confidence in themselves and their supporters ; it necessarily intimidates
friends, as it certainly stimulates and encourages opposition."

Mr. Adams was charged with being imprudent in his
communications which reached the public. Thus on
the *ebony and topaz* business, Hammond pours out his
feelings to Mr. Clay:

" I wish Mr. Adams's *ebony and topaz* were submerged

in the deepest profound of the bathos. You great men have no privilege to commit blunders. You belong to others whom you can not always consult, and whom it is not always safe to confide in. I had said to myself, Mr. Adams wrote for Walsh the article on the Colonial trade, and I am resolved to have him in high estimation, and here comes this (I have no name for it) to mar all my resolutions. Is there no hope for Walsh? I wish he were pleased or would go over to the enemy."

The whole business lacked the spirit and passion of party. Yet let it not be supposed that the evil of office-seeking had yet tempted any to attempt a departure from the methods of a constitutional civil service. Hammond, on behalf of the good citizens of Ohio, expressed their preference for the appointment of a competent and reputable man for district attorney, and suggested the propriety of the Representatives joining in the recommendation. There was no soliciting from a Senatorial Boss—a Boss Roscoe, Boss Don, or Boss Jack, for the Senate then considered nominations to office, sitting as a court, and had not usurped the function of appointment conferred by the Constitution upon the President. The necessities of the bosses have worked a revolutionary change in the fundamental law which originally contemplated the dignity of the executive and the rights of the people. Now the power and the dignity and the rights are all embraced in the Senatorial office.

We have reached the last Presidential contest between Adams and Jackson. The scheme of opposition which had been formed originally had been pursued with hard persistence for three years—three years of falsehood, blackguardism, and violence, as well as of idiotic adulation of a man possessed of some good, and many bad traits, but who had had the fortune to defend New Orleans and defeat the British. Around him gathered the corrupt and vicious, and waged a war of defamation against upright statesmen. Jackson was herein the leader, as he was in all movements with which he was connected. He shrewdly understood the advantage of constantly pressing his enemy. "Say what you will," wrote Hammond, "these Jacksonians are excellent politicians." And so they were, if the word "excellent," may be interpretated to mean shrewd, cunning, false, and malicious.

"I assert," said McDuffie, "and am willing to stake my humble stock of reputation upon the truth of the assertion, that the circumstances of the extraordinary coalition between Adams and Clay, furnish as strong evidence of an abandonment of political principle on the part of Mr. Clay, and of a corrupt political bargain between him and Mr. Adams, as is ordinarily required to establish the guilt of those who are charged in a Court of Quarter Sessions with the common crimes known to the law."

This published in the Heroite prints, and in the Jacobin Clubs, and reiterated in every gin shop, made a great impression on the people. Against it only the simple facts could be related. But

"Truth lies entrapped where cunning finds no bar."

There was one friend of the administration who had the courage to face this clamorous horde and assail their leader single handed. In November, 1827, Hammond wrote Mr. Clay :

"I send you the prospectus of a new work, intended to be conducted with spirit, and calculated to travel into all the by-ways of politics. It will be adapted to the meridian of Ohio, Indiana, and Illinois, and not unsuited to Pennsylvania. If the press can effect any thing we are determined to do what we can in that way."

The title of this unique campaign paper was "Truth's Advocate," which Hammond edited in addition to his practice at the Bar and work on the Gazette. It was an extraordinary paper. "It was terribly severe on Jackson," says Mr. Mansfield, in his Memoirs, "chiefly because it was truth that it stated and proved. But of what value is truth when opposed to human passions?" The historical articles on Jackson's military career, his arbitrary conduct, despotic character, and illegal marriage provoked Jackson to retaliatory measures. He threatened to challenge Clay and force a duel. This phase will be explained by the following letters:

CLAY TO HAMMOND.

WASHINGTON, *December* 23, 1826.

(Confidential.)

DEAR SIR:

I had a curious call the day before yesterday from Major Eaton. He came at the instance of General Jackson to inform me that the General had received a letter from some person in Kentucky (whose name was not given), communicating to him that you had, during your visit to Kentucky, last summer, obtained from *me* papers which I had collected for the purpose of an attack on Mrs. Jackson which you were preparing; and to inquire if I had furnished any such papers. As there was not a particle of truth in the communication which had been made to the General, I, of course, contradicted it, adding what is perfectly true that I had never seen the papers relating to the transaction referred to, nor did I know that you had on your above-mentioned visit procured any such papers. I stated that I saw you in Lexington a day or two, and that I understood when you left it you passed by Paris to visit Judge Trimble on your return home.

I have now no recollection that the case of Mrs. Jackson formed any topic of conversation between us when you were in Lexington. I do recollect that you mentioned something about a suit in chancery concerning the purchase of the press in Lexington, and that you had obtained a copy of the bill, etc.

The session so far remains calm. In what quarter the storm of opposition will burst forth can only now be a matter of conjecture. I think it will be the British colonial question, on what, if I am not greatly deceived, you will agree with me in thinking that the administration stands on perfectly impregnable ground.

The subject of the Vice-Presidency begins to engage conversation. My name, I find, is spoken of by some.

I confess my judgment leans against its use. What is your opinion?

I am yours with great regard.

4

HAMMOND TO EATON.

CINCINNATI, *January 3,* 1827.

SIR :

I am advised information has been communicated to General Jackson that Mr. Clay had furnished me with certain documents in relation to Mrs. Jackson, upon which I was preparing an attack on her. I deem it an act of justice to say to you that this information is wholly incorrect. I never received from Mr. Clay any paper or document upon that subject ; it was never but once a subject of conversation between us. According to my present recollection, from my earliest knowledge of General Jackson's character, I had heard exception taken to the manner in which his connubial relation was commenced. I had heard various stories with respect to it. At Columbus, in the summer of 1824, I enquired of Mr. Clay what was the true state of facts. He stated that he knew nothing but by report. The relation he gave was palliatory, and he expressed his opinion that the subject ought not to be brought before the public. I mentioned this conversation to Colonel Andrew Mack, of this city, on our return from Columbus, who is now and was then a warm supporter of General Jackson for the Presidency, and he expressed himself entirely satisfied with the conduct of Mr. Clay.

It has been for some time my opinion that this matter should be investigated, and I set on foot an inquiry to obtain the information that would enable me to decide, for myself, at least, how far the public were interested in it. From Mr. Edward Day, a traveling collector for merchants of Baltimore, I obtained reference to the petition of Roberts for a divorce, addressed to the Virginia Legislature in 1790; the act that was passed by that body December 20th of the same year, and the judicial proceedings founded upon it, in Mercer county, Kentucky. What use I shall make of these documents, and the facts connected with them, must depend upon future events. I meditate no attack upon Mrs. Jackson. I do not view the character of the General in a light so favorable as you and many others do; and I propose to use this affair in no other manner than to elucidate my estimate of that character. I wish to shun no proper responsibility, and should I make any publication, it will be accompanied with my name.

This letter is addressed to you in a spirit of frankness to prevent any misconception of my intention, and any mistake as to the channels through which I derived my information.

Respectfully yours, etc.,

(To John H. Eaton, Esq.)   C. HAMMOND.

One purpose Hammond had in view in reciting the story of the Hero's life, was accomplished: Jackson drew off his dogs for a time and the administration had a few weeks of peace.

A glance at "Truth's Advocate" may not prove unacceptable. Besides the telling exposition of Jackson's career of blood and violence, there are thoughtful and able discussions of public affairs, and the qualifications requisite in an administrator of civil government, and many flashes of wit and humor interspersed. Among the lighter papers, a drama in five acts, entitled "The Hero of two Wars," well pays a reading. The verse is much above the average of such productions, the wit is capital, and the political characterizations accurate. The characters are Hero, Lady Hero, Antiquary (Caleb Atwater), Toady (Lee), Director (Van Buren), Outcast (Aaron Burr), Cypher, Orator Puff, citizens, messengers, and ghosts, the latter seven in number, representing the shades of the seven, including Harris, the Baptist preacher, whose violent deaths Jackson was responsible for. The drama opens—scene, an inn at the capitol—with Hero soliloquizing and plotting for the overthrow of Adams and Clay :

> *Hero:* Kremer, importing charge of vile intrigue,
> Corruption, management, and base design,
> Against the opposers of my great intent,
> Has laid the corner-stone on which I'll build
> The glorious edifice of future fame.
> Born in the tempest of tumultuous war,
> I relish not this " piping times of peace ;"
> Hero must be foremost or be nothing,
> Sink to oblivion, and be known no more,
> " Or mount the whirlwind and direct the storm."
> Propitious now the season to begin,
> I'll fan the spark of slander's fiery brand,
> Until I'll wrap the nation in a flame
> That shall consume my foes, though they were pure
> As min'st'ring angels from the realms of light.
>   *   *   *   *   *   *
> The disaffected first I'll conjure up.
> Mischief! how apt a counsellor art thou,
> For now thou dost remind me of a wretch
> Whom once his country at her bar arraigned
> For deep conspiracy against the state.
> And though he 'scaped the meshes of the law,
> Yet dark suspicion fastened on his name,
> For which he bears that country deadly hate.

This person, of course, is Burr, to whom the Hero writes and dispatches the letter by a messenger, and then adds :

> He wants no prompter
> But his strong revenge—no spur to action,
> But his, and kindred spirits aggrandisement.
> Thus will I start the quarry, and the pack
> Of hungry office-hunters will join in,
> And raise the general clamor of the chase.

The portrait of Van Buren and his attempt to over-reach Aaron Burr, is a clever piece of work. I can read but two or three passages :

Van Buren is introduced as Director. He is not prepared to trust the Hero, without further information as to his faithfulness to political pledges. If this is favorable, he resolves to accept the trust and become Hero's manager. He decides to go and consult Outcast (Burr).

> He knows this chieftain well—has fully proved him ;
> His nerves, his faith, his mighty master passion,
> Have all been probed ; their deep and secret working
> Drawn to the surface, and made bare before him.
> The times are in conjunction too, with Outcast ;
> His friends are in repute, and he looks upward :
> A second Marius from the dust of Afric,
> Rising to wreak his vengeance on his country,
> And die with gloating joy, a bloody dotard.
> His hopes are in full action, and awake him
> To old ambitions and deep smothered vengeance.
> 'Tis long since he were soothed with courtier-language,
> 'Twill steal upon his soul, as I shall use it—
> Oh thou ! the subtle genius, by whose aid
> I have threaded the dark maze of policy,

In all its crooked windings, and have reached
The lofty pinnacle on which I stand !
Inspire me now with Machiavelian skill ;
Grant that the bland, insinuating smile
In all its softest tints may rest upon me ;
Let every look evince sincerity,
And every motive seem as undisguised
As maiden's blushes at a tale of love.
Give me the eye of Argus : let me hear
As with a thousand ears : let nought escape me,
For now the crisis of my fate approaches,
I rise to power, or fall to rise no more.

Scene shifts again, a parlor in which is Outcast seated. Cypher enters and informs him that Director seeks a private interview.

Outcast.—With me, and does not name the object of it ?
Cypher.—He does so ; and he says he has good reasons,
Which, when disclosed, you will appreciate.
He speaks you fairly, as it is his wont,
When he would serve himself by others' aid.
Matters of high import, of deep concernment,
To you, your friends ; thus he speaks :
Smiles graciously, and grasps the yielding palm,
Presses it softly, looking wondrous things.

Outcast knows his man and reads him unerringly. He resolves to expose him and teach him a lesson in the art of the crafty politician. He consents to see Director, and appoints an hour and place of meeting. He sends word to his associates to meet him at the appointed place, where they lie concealed, and appear at a given signal to the confusion of Director.

Last scene.—A chamber dimly lighted. I wish I could give you this scene entire. As a subtle piece of wit and character delineating, it is well worth reading. The old politician outshines the new in blandishments, and outwits him in craft. At a signal his witnesses appear, but the Director, although knowing that he is caught, preserves a calm exterior. He greets the friends cordially as compatriots banded in the common cause.

" Give me your hands ; I hope to know you better.
   The fiat shall go forth.   The mouthing herd,
   The hurrah boys, can not be safely trusted.
   Power must be wrested from them, and confided
   To our kindred spirits who will wield it,
   To place our chieftain in the highest seat.
   Success is never treason.   My humble board,
   My services are all at your command ;
   Time moves apace.   My honored friends, adieu."
   (*Exit Director, smiling and bowing gracefully.*)
   Outcast.—And this man passes for a deep intriguer !
   The times indeed are altered.   Can it be
   The great Magician,* my once hated rival,
   Was duped by such a caitiff?
   Cypher—Nothing more certain ; but his powers were
      sinking,
   And death removed him from the humiliation,
   As in compassion of his former greatness.
   Toady.—'T is useless to disparage the Director.
   Say what you may, he's a well spoken man,
   A polished gentleman—his easy manner,
   His sweet insinuating smile, his bow,
   The pressure of his hand, his every motion,
   Steal on the good opinion of his friends—
   He's almost Hero's equal in the graces.

The reflections of Outcast need not be rehearsed. He is sure of outwitting the Director in case of Hero's

---

* Alexander Hamilton.

election. When, he exclaims, was a southern nabob ruled by Low Dutch cunning!

Towards the close of Mr. Adams' administration, the President tendered to Clay a position on the Supreme Bench—a fact communicated to Hammond in one of those confidential letters Mr. Clay was wont to write to him. Later, this appointment was tendered to Mr. Hammond, and was declined. In my opinion it was declined because the place had first been offered to another. Hammond knew that he was better fitted for a judicial position than Clay, and he knew, too, that his great services merited high recognition. I know the friends of Hammond assign another reason, but the correspondence to which I have referred to-night, and human nature confirm my opinion. It is true Hammond refused all political honors, but the Bench was his place, and there his great talents would have shown brilliantly. In 1829, the correspondence between Clay and Hammond ceased, and was not renewed until 1832, after the nomination at Baltimore. During this and the following year, the great editor with characteristic independence, wrote a series of articles to show that the strength of Jacksonism was so great, a new policy should be adopted, and the old leaders retired. This gave offense to Clay. In 1832, Hammond wrote Clay a manly letter vindicating his independence. One passage is worth our attention : " My life," wrote he, " has been devoted to politics rather as a master passion, than from any yearning of the most honorable ambition. I have never wished or sought public employment, either for the pecuniary reward, or that of distinction. Though always an ardent actor, I felt myself a disinterested one, and have therefore (not very modestly perhaps) claimed to be a more impartial judge of surrounding prospects than others of equal experience."

Mr. Hammond had found a new favorite, and one with tastes in harmony with his own. "I am much gratified to mark how rapidly Mr. Webster is growing in public estimation. That such a man acquires a permanent popularity, as he becomes better known, is highly creditable to the good sense of the community. In my view it is a redeeming trait in the character of a people sufficient to atone for very many aberrations." This was in 1826. Later, he submitted to Mr. Webster, a plan for the reorganization of the courts.

Hammond had formed a much higher opinion of Mr. Adams, whose motives in political action he had come to understand better. I am tempted to read to you a letter from Mr. Adams after he had retired from office, but our brief time will not admit of it.

The history of the effort to crush out the freedom of speech and the press in America in the interest of the slave-holders of the Southern States, is full of exciting interest and deep humiliation. You are familiar with the Virginia Bill of rights drawn by George Mason, and the fact of the opposition to the adoption of the Federal Constitution by Southern Statesmen, because a similar clause had not been incorporated in that instrument. Either these distinguished gentlemen were mere theorists or their successors were degenerate in a love of liberty. Most conspicuous in the Virginia Constitution during these years whose events we are considering, was this clause:

"The freedom of the press is one of the great bulwarks of liberty, and can never be restrained but by despotic governments."

We have seen that Charles Hammond freely discussed the slavery question in its relations to government and society for years, while being a leader of his party and intimately associated with Mr. Clay. The influence of his pen was widely felt. We have seen how Hayne, White, and others, demanded that all discussions, and all negotations affecting slavery, should cease. In time other men came to the front, who were not content to abide by constitutional rights, or rely on a firm assertion of the same, but who, holding that slavery was a sin, proclaimed a crusade against the Constitution itself. The combined commercial and political power of the South was exerted, after 1830, to crush out agitation with remarkable vigor. The general acquiescence on the part of the North was no less remarkable. The moral degradation, and the subserviency to party must have been great when a President could recommend in an annual message, the exclusion from the mails of anti-slavery litera-ature; and when his Postmaster-General openly encouraged the rifling of the public mail. And yet these things were done under the administration of Andrew Jackson.

The logical result of all this was a resort to mob violence, and the attempted forcible suppression of the freedom of speech. Hammond continues his manly assertion of constitutional rights, and in this way is surely quickening the conscience, self-respect, and manhood of the North which in time shall be overwhelming. His soul is moved as never before. He strikes ponderous blows. He is indignant at the subserviency of the

North. The radiant humor that has heretofore characterized his editorials, gives place to sarcasm and fierce denunciation. The Methodist General Conference of the West met and resolved that the church was opposed to modern abolitionism, and disclaimed any purpose to interfere between master and slave. Hammond's comment was brief but effective: "What strange revolutions of feelings and sentiment are produced in which just principles bear no part! If, at the General Conference of 1828, it could have been suggested that such a proceeding could have been had at the General Conference of 1836, every member would have indignantly exclaimed: 'Are we dogs that we should do this thing?'"

To those who demanded that agitation should cease because slavery was recognized in the Constitution, he replied with crushing force: "It is said the Constitution has secured slave property, and now none should argue against it. Yes, the Constitution has secured it, and how? By never naming it. By a kind of shamefaced endurance of it! But the Constitution has secured freedom of speech by a broad, strong, explicit declaration, and now collision has arisen between that which is barely tolerated as an admitted curse, and that which is asserted as an essential good, viz.: 'Freedom of speech and of the press.'"

James G. Birney, Gamaliel Bailey, Dr. Colby, and others, had established a press in Cincinnati, under the direction of the Anti-Slavery Society of Ohio. The Philanthropist newspaper had Achiles Pugh for printer and publisher. These are familiar names. In the summer of 1836, there was an active agitation in the community against the publication of this paper, which culminated in a citizens' meeting in Lower Market, and the appointment of a committee to endeavor to secure its suppression by peaceful means. On that committee were such distinguished citizens as Judge Jacob Burnet, Nicholas Longworth, Morgan Neville, John C. Wright, Wm. Greene, David T. Disney, Robert Buchanan, and John P. Foote. These gentlemen represented to Mr. Birney and his associates that the publication of the Philanthropist would drive away the Southern trade, and ruin the property interests of the city, and begged them to desist. This being refused, a mob under the direction of the mayor, took possession of the city for two days and nights, destroyed the presses and office of Mr. Pugh, destroyed the residences of several inoffensive colored people, and established a reign of terror. During the progress of the storm, Mr. Hammond called a few citizens together at the Gazette office, and arranged for a public meeting at the court-house of the friends of law and order and the Constitution. The call bears the names of forty well known citizens, including Charles Hammond, W. D. Gallagher, and Salmon P. Chase, the latter a young man then preparing for the great part he was afterwards to take in public affairs. When these law and order citizens and friends of the Constitution went to the court-house, they found a meeting already organized in the interest of the other side. The only way to reach the public was through the columns of the Gazette. Mr. Hammond made a public statement, and in it included what he had prepared for adoption at the meeting.

The spirit of it will be understood from the follow-ing paragraph :

" We regard slavery as a domestic institution of the states in which it exists, with which the other states have no right to interfere. But while we respect the rights of our fellow-citizens of the slave-holding states, and would, by no means, break through or suffer any others to break through the sacred barriers of the law for the purpose of invading those rights; we also respect the rights of our fellow-citizens of the non-slave-holding states, and will never suffer the law and Constitution to be trampled in the dust for the purpose of destroying those rights. Among these rights—and of all the dear-est, because it is the bulwark of all the rest, is the right of FREE DISCUSSION—the right of every citizen to write, speak, and print upon every subject as he may think proper, being responsible to the laws and the laws ONLY, for the abuse of that liberty. If this right shall perish through the violence of a mob, the grave that entombs it must be the sepulchre of American freedom. True-hearted Americans, therefore, must defend this right at all times, in all places, under all circumstances, by whomsoever assailed. When this right is abused, the remedy is at hand. The courts are open. If the ex-isting laws do not provide an efficient remedy, let new laws, adapted to the object, be enacted. The annual sessions of our Legislature are held for that purpose. But let not the hand of violence be raised against the exercise of this precious right. However obnoxious the exercise may be, let the right itself be acknowledged and respected. Let us not for the sake of removing

some unsightly blemish, pull out the very corner-stone
of the great temple of constitutional liberty."

Hammond's calm statement exasperated the desperate
men in control of the city.   They sent bullies to attack
him and threaten his life, and mobs with tar and
feathers to terrify him, but these he faced with splendid
courage, and single and alone drove them before him—
the cowardly scullions !   A night raid on the Gazette
office was organized, but the sight of that brave man
scattered the mob.

The successive issues of the Gazette for several days
had no editorial comments, but instead, contained that
chapter from Job, in which the just man says :

" Let the day perish wherein I was born, and the
night in which it was said, 'there is a man child con-
ceived.' "

Passages from the Declaration of Independence, the
Constitution, and the Ordinance of 1787, bearing on the
freedom of speech and the press.   A contemporary, an
eloquent divine, says that the citizens concerned in the
disgraceful events I have described, afterwards attempted
to destroy the records of their shame, and that the
Gazette for July 24, 1836, was removed from the
library files.   After the civil war had destroyed slavery,
he referred to Hammond's work in these words :
" Since now no wind on this mighty continent bears
on its wings the sigh of a slave, or will bear one forever, let Charles Hammond's biography be written.
Let our children's children declaim his sentences.   Let
their prize orations paint him at that darkest hour of
the Republic, far darker than the darkest battle-day of
the war, standing here at the commercial head-quarters

of slavery, and standing alone against the brutal terrors of mobs by which many fell ; against aristocratic threats and hatred ; against children weeping and entreating ; against the diabolical ferocities of caste ; against the fulminations of the sanhedrims of Protestantism ; against mercantile avarice and greed ; against all his political enemies and associates ; yet standing at the wheel when all the timbers below him were cracking and giving way ; the fragments of three abolition presses broken by mobs lying round his feet; driven back, absolutely pushed out of his own editorial chair, retreating behind the Bible, the Declaration of Independence, the Bill of Rights, and by the sole force of his integrity and truth, filling the assailants of freedom and justice with such terror, as to drive them to seek the shelter of oblivion, by destroying the records of that day."

Mobs at Alton, mobs at Boston, and mobs at Philadelphia, are also notable events. But these are chiefly exhibitions of passion aroused by prejudice and ignorance. Far different were the scenes enacted in Congress during this, the midnight of the American dark age. In the House of Representatives, surrounded by men whose faces indicated fierce passions and intense hate, there stood a man day after day, and week after week, defending and upholding the Constitution, asserting the right of petition, and the freedom of debate—to my eyes the noblest figure ever seen in the American Congress, and one of the noblest and grandest ever seen in parliament of men in any country—this Old Man Eloquent, then and there in the nineteenth century, representing the conscience and manhood yet alive in the nation. As for myself, I can not think of this struggle for constitutional principles without emotion, and a feeling of thankfulness that, under divine Providence, America was then blessed with men of courage and wisdom and patriotism like John Quincy Adams and Charles Hammond. I can not look upon the cramped handwriting of these letters which tell the story of the struggle for freedom, without a feeling of reverence for this the noblest of all the Adamses. He was the superior man contending for righteousness in the midst of " the thieves of virtue." Possessing that sublime courage, unerring vision, and largeness of soul, that distinguishes the man of action from his fellows. It is profitable to dwell on this scene. A man who has enjoyed the highest honors, pos-sessed of wealth, and invited to the comforts of leisure, filling a lower station, surrounded by warring elements, and of these, he only comprehending the danger to the Republic. Will he to the rescue?

" On a sudden, from the opposite side of the hori-zon, see, miraculous Opportunity, rushing hitherward —swift, terrible, clothed with lightning like a courser of the gods ;—dare he clutch *him* by the thunder-mane, and fling himself upon him, and make for the Empy-rean by that course rather? Then must he be quick about it ; the time is now or never ! "

The deed is done ! Freedom of the press, the right of petition, are saved to the citizens, and under their blessed influence in time, Liberty and Union do be-come one and indivisible.

Fifteen years before Adams, Hammond was discuss-ing these very principles. He now rejoices that a voice is heard in the Halls of Congress, proclaiming the truth. He says, in the Gazette, February 16, 1837 :

"The course of J. Q. Adams, in Congress, on the subject of presenting abolition petitions, has been censured by some. It meets my unqualified approbation. I rejoice that there is one man in Congress who has the boldness to stand up for what is right; the firmness to maintain his ground against denunciation; the talent to sustain himself, though assailed by violence on one side and meanly deserted by cowardly skulkers on the other. . . .

"Mr. Adams is avowedly no abolitionist. He plants himself upon the right of petition; upon the right of every citizen to present his grievances for hearing and redress to a legislative body whom the petitioner honestly supposes may act upon his case.

. . . "The Constitution of the United States secures the right of petition. The provision is found in the first amendment; that amendment originated in Virginia, and is in these words:"

(Here follows the amendment.)

"The right to petition is here secured in connection with the right to enjoy religious opinion and the freedom of speech and of the press. Thus, this right of petition is arranged with, and noted as one of the great fundamental rights of freemen. Mr. Adams does nothing but maintain this right in presenting abolition petitions. In the uproar raised by Southern members of Congress against receiving these petitions, there is a direct attempt to subvert a constitutional right. I venerate the man who distinguishes between the unwise use of a right on one side, and an unconstitutional effort to subvert that right on the other: who plants himself in

5

the breach, between fanaticism and usurpation, and regardless of consequences does his duty.

> "'In Freedom's field, advancing his firm foot,
> He plants it on the line that Justice draws,
> And will prevail or perish in her cause.'"

Then follows an argument on the duty of Congress to act on the subject of slavery in several particulars, which are specified, and the powers of that body under the Constitution. Mr. Hammond concludes in these words:

"In respect to abolition petitions, the South has assumed an unconstitutional attitude. She denies the right to petition. She denounces the exercise of the right, and she contemns members of Congress, who differently regard their constitutional obligations, as no better than incendiaries. Mr. Adams, in the true spirit of those who threw the tea into the water, says:

"'Nay, gentlemen, I take no sides with these petitioners. I disapprove their object, but they have rights under the Constitution, and they ask me to assert these rights here in their behalf, and I do so. I regret to give you offense. I more than regret the fury you manifest; but I can not swerve from the performance of a duty which I feel that I owe to the Constitution and to the rights of a fellow-citizen, however injudiciously asserted.' In this light I regard the course of Mr. Adams, that has recently brought upon him so much opprobrium. Thus viewing it, I deem it my duty, as *I feel it my privilege*, to express my opinion in relation to it. Were I a member of Congress I should be glad to stand by Mr. Adams in the contest in which

he is engaged.   Regardless who are the petitioners, or
what the object, if the one be respectful, and Congress
can have power over the other, I would never shrink
from their presentation, or be driven, unless by brute
force, from maintaining the right to present them."

Mr. Adams acknowledged the help he had received
in this letter, the chirography of which is so cramped as
to require to be written out before it could be publicly
read :

Adams to Hammond.

Washington, *March* 31, 1837.

Dear Sir :

In the severe trial through which I was destined to
pass, during the session of Congress now closed,
nothing occurred more cheering and encouraging to me
than the notices taken of the debates in your paper, and
your friendly letter of the 16th of February.

The abolition of slavery in the District of Columbia,
in the purpose of the petitioners for it, is a *step* towards
the abolition throughout the Union of the Institution
of Domestic Slavery—and indeed throughout the world.
The object is noble—the motive pure—but the under-
taking of such tremendous magnitude, difficulty, and
danger, that I shrink from the contemplation of it, and
much more from any personal agency in promoting it.
I have abstained, sometimes perhaps too pertinaciously
abstained, from all participation in measures *leading* to
that conflict for life and death between *Freedom* and
Slavery, through which I have not yet been able to see
how this Union could ultimately be preserved from
passing.   While the people of the Slave-holding States

professed the speculative opinions upon the subject of slavery, of which Mr. Jefferson was the principal promulgator, I had flattered myself that slavery was in this Union gradually perishing with a marasmus, and that its dissolution and interment might be left to those of whose constitutions it formed a part. This hope I was encouraged to entertain by the continual progress of the spirit of emancipation, manifested by the abolition of the African slave trade, spreading all over Europe, and enacted by our own Congress, even before I thought they were authorized by the Constitution of the United States to exercise that legislative power; by the earnestness with which Great Britain was pursuing the policy of emancipation, and by the co-operation, apparently cordial, which our government under slave-holding Presidents, was yielding to that policy. But the consequences of the emancipation by Great Britain of all her slaves in the West Indies, with the abolition of slavery in all the new South American Republics, on the one hand, and of the Southampton insurrection, and the subsequent debates in the Legislature of Virginia on the other, have gone far towards bringing my hopes to a pause. Since then, the spirit of universal emancipation has been ripening into a religious principle, fortified with unanswerable logic, stimulated by the fervor of conscience, and armed with the irrepressible energies of martyrdom. On the other hand slavery, driven from her strongholds of power, has changed her tone and become a reasoner. Professor Dew, of William and Mary College, Virginia, Chancellor Harper, and Governor McDuffie, of South Carolina, have become the founders of a new school of political morality for Republics founded upon the Declaration of Independence, and the unalienable rights of man. Their first principle is that the negro is an inferior race, neither possessing nor entitled to the rights of man, but born for servitude, and destined to it as long as this globe shall last. That this degradation of the African black, was intended by the Creator, for the express benefit of the white *Anglo-Saxon*, for his temporal and spiritual improvement in wisdom, virtue, and especially freedom, and that your negro-driver is the only man upon earth who understands and practices the true principles of liberty.

These doctrines, with the atrocious aggravations of oppression in the recent sharpening of the Draconian black code of our Southern States, with their demands upon the free States to deliver up their citizens to their revenge, and upon Congress to strangle the circulation of free thought by the mails, have, I confess, moved my indignation, and sometimes provoked me to think it time to try their temper in turn. Yet, so strong has been the current of popular feeling in all the free States, to support the slavery of the South, and against the Abolitionists, that when I found myself almost the only man in the House who dared ever to present their petitions, they crowded upon me in such multitudes, that for merely presenting them I brought all the resentments of the South upon me without even a prospect of support from my own constituents, representing as I did, a district where the abolition cause is in special disfavor. The articles in your paper were almost my only support in the House, and the blind fury of the nullification party which took the lead for the South in in the House broke them down there.

Presidential electioneering, remote as well as present, makes up a false issue against the Abolitionists, in all the free States, where alone they are permitted even to exist. For the first time since the existence of the Constitution of the United States, the election of a President has turned exclusively upon the slavery and abolition conflict. It is the only point upon which the new President has declared his fixed and irrevocable determination in advance. Is not our whole political system irresistibly tending to turn upon that hinge alone? I am deeply apprehensive that it is.

I took the pen only to thank you for the articles in your Gazette, on my trial, and for your kind letter; and tender you my respectful salutations and good wishes.

J. Q. ADAMS.

(Charles Hammond, Esq., Cincinnati, O.)

The lateness of the hour warns me to bring my address to a close. I pass by the subsequent discussions in which Mr. Adams and Mr. Hammond are concerned, and turn to a new scene, in which Henry Clay is the central figure.

"What a loud-roaring, loose and empty matter," says Carlyle, "is this tornado of vociferation which men call 'Public Opinion!'"

True. But we have seen what tremendous power it had in these dark days, and how only a very few refused to be silent. It presses Mr. Clay so hard that he consents to come to the front as the apologist and defender of the Southern view. The hope of the Presidency is, alas! greater than the love of truth and the aspiration to do right in the sight of God.

Mr. Hammond is called on to publicly criticise his old friend, which he does fearlessly and most thoroughly in a series of nine editorials. He is in feeble health; the beckonings from the Silent Land are now discernible, and he can leave his house but seldom. All of his strength is husbanded to perform a few duties of deep concernment to others and to his country, which he has loved with such fervid, unselfish patriotism; and this protest against the utterances of his life-long friend is one of them. The editorials appeared at intervals during a period of two months immediately following Mr. Clay's speech.

It would be a vain task to attempt to describe these articles which embrace the best thoughts of the patriot whose light is nearly out. Mr. Clay quickly heard of them, and in a touching note, from Washington, asked his old friend to send him copies as they appeared.

Towards the close, Hammond, in a tone of sadness, considers the effect of the influence of the great name of his friend, now used freely by the enemies of the Constitution—the old Constitution of freedom as they once both read it—but he warns him that even this will suffice only for a season: that the South are seeking to crush out rights founded upon divine law that will surely be vindicated in the future.

" I say the opponents of slavery *must* be heard. The great question of human liberty in this land can not be decided by the denunciation of masters, the accommodations of trade, or the impulsive violence of infuri-

ated men.   Mr. Clay himself can not effect this.   The
effort he has made, strong as it is, must fail in compro-
mitting to his views the slavery antagonists of the land.
Their passive deference to his behests, can not be pressed
too far."

   " Has all discretion," asked Hammond, on another
occasion, "deserted the owners of slaves?   Do they
suppose that blood liable to be heated flows in no veins
but their own ?   One day they must learn otherwise."

   With this warning, and the light of this prophecy
streaming into the future, I close this very imperfect
record of the life-work of Charles Hammond, who, for
over forty years, was one of the Republic's ablest, most
unselfish, and most faithful sons, and a witness to the
spirit and principles of government as established by
the Fathers.

www.ingramcontent.com/pod-product-compliance
Lightning Source LLC
Chambersburg PA
CBHW030023030726
47499CB00008B/3090